BLACK
ACHIEVEMENTS

IN BUSINESS

**CELEBRATING OPRAH WINFREY,
MOZIAH BRIDGES, AND MORE**

ROBERT P. DIXON JR.
CICELY LEWIS, EXECUTIVE EDITOR

Lerner Publications ◆ Minneapolis

LETTER FROM CICELY LEWIS

Dear Reader,

As a girl, I wanted to be like Oprah Winfrey. She is a Black woman from Mississippi like me who became an award-winning actor, author, and businessperson. Oftentimes, history books leave out the accomplishments and contributions of people of color. When you

CICELY LEWIS

see someone who looks like you and has a similar background excelling at something, it helps you to see yourself be great.

I created Read Woke to amplify the voices of people who are often underrepresented. These books bring to light the beauty, talent, and integrity of Black people in music, activism, sports, the arts, and other areas. As you read, think about why it's important to celebrate Black excellence and the achievements of all people regardless of race, gender, or status. How did the people mentioned succeed despite barriers placed on them? How can we use these stories to inspire others?

Black excellence is everywhere in your daily life. I hope these people inspire you to never give up and continue to let your light shine.

With gratitude,

Cicely Lewis

TABLE OF CONTENTS

CREATING BLACK POWER AND WEALTH

Clarence O. Smith, Cecil Hollingsworth, Jonathan Blount, Denise M. Clark, and Edward Lewis founded the media company Essence Communications Inc. in 1968. The first issue of *Essence* magazine came out in 1970. The magazine printed about fifty thousand copies per month and celebrated Black culture, fashion, and entertainment. By 2022 the company reached over twenty million people through its magazine, website, and events. CEO Caroline A. Wanga heads its leadership team, composed entirely of Black women.

The success of *Essence* magazine and the company's team shows how Black business owners create paths to economic freedom that can last for generations. From restaurants to fashion lines, Black business owners in the US develop products and services that reflect their cultural history. They also invest in the community by supporting youth groups, community building, and civil rights.

This book will profile Black excellence in business. Although it cannot include all successful Black business owners, it features several from a variety of businesses.

Business owners might work in many different settings.

Oprah Winfrey with students the year before she launched the Oprah Winfrey Leadership Academy for Girls

CHAPTER 1

POWERFUL BLACK BILLIONAIRES

Black business owners use their creativity to build business empires. Some have even become billionaires. They can use their wealth to make a difference in people's lives.

FAMOUS TV PERSONALITY AND PHILANTHROPIST

Oprah Winfrey is a gifted speaker. This made *The Oprah Winfrey Show* the highest-rated talk show in the United States. Her show aired nationally from 1986 until 2011. Oprah is also an award-winning actor. She appeared in several films and a television miniseries. She was a voice actor in animated films, including *Princess and the Frog* and *Charlotte's Web*.

Oprah became a billionaire in 2003. She supports education and community building worldwide. In 2007 she launched a $40 million school for girls in South Africa. By 2022, 528 girls had graduated from the Oprah Winfrey Leadership Academy for Girls.

Oprah interviewing actor Hugh Jackman on her talk show in 2010

DID YOU KNOW?

Actor and filmmaker Tyler Perry went from being without a home to live in to being a self-made billionaire. His first play was performed before a nearly empty theater. But he continued to produce plays and movies. His first film, *Diary of a Mad Black Woman*, earned around $22 million in its first weekend in theaters in 2005.

Tyler Perry received a star on the Hollywood Walk of Fame in 2019.

BUILDING A BILLION-DOLLAR BUSINESS

Reginald F. Lewis was a lawyer, business leader, and philanthropist. He started his career as a corporate lawyer on Wall Street in 1968. In 1983 he founded a venture capital company. He bought another company, Beatrice Foods, and built it into the first Black-owned business to make over a billion dollars a year. In 1993 *Forbes* magazine listed him as one of the four hundred richest Americans.

Lewis created the Reginald F. Lewis Foundation in 1987 to invest millions of dollars in communities. It supports education, arts, and social justice. He challenged others to never stop pursuing their dreams.

After Reginald F. Lewis's death, his foundation donated $5 million to help build the Reginald F. Lewis Museum of Maryland African American History and Culture.

MAKING DREAMS COME TRUE

Robert F. Smith worked hard to make his dreams come true while helping others achieve theirs. In high school, he found a passion for computer science. He tried to apply for an internship at Bell Labs, a research and technology company. It was only for college students, but he called the company every week for months. He was selected for the internship and continued working there during college.

Smith went on to build a successful career and become a billionaire. He used his money to invest in communities. While

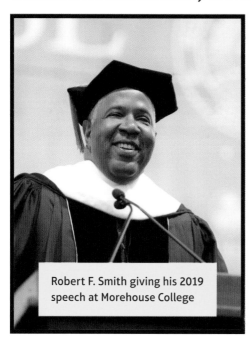

Robert F. Smith giving his 2019 speech at Morehouse College

giving a speech at Morehouse College in 2019, Smith pledged to donate $34 million to pay off the debt of nearly four hundred graduates. He was also the first African American to sign the Giving Pledge, agreeing to donate half his net worth during his lifetime.

REFLECT

What skills do you need to be an effective business owner?

Lisa Price (*left*), the owner of beauty brand Carol's Daughter, looks at her beauty products with DJ Jazzy Joyce in 2007.

CHAPTER 2

PIONEERS IN HAIR AND FASHION

Hairstyles and fashion are sources of pride and creative expression in the Black community and reflect their cultural roots. Each style is unique. Black leaders have built businesses to meet their communities' hair-care and fashion needs. They inspire trends and unite communities through style.

SUCCESS MADE IN THE KITCHEN

Lisa Price created Carol's Daughter, a beauty company, in 1993. She began by creating natural hair-care products for all hair types in her kitchen. She named her company Carol's Daughter to honor her relationship with her mother, Carol. Her company grew from humble beginnings to a national brand. She shared her business journey in her 2004 book, *Success Never Smelled So Sweet*.

In 2017 Price was featured in an exhibit at the Smithsonian National Museum of African American History and Culture. A jar of her Healthy Hair Butter was displayed as part of the Cultural Expressions exhibit. Her products are sold in popular stores nationwide. In 2020 she sold her company to L'Oreal USA. At the time, Carol's Daughter was worth about $27 million.

Price posing with some of her Carol's Daughter products

DID YOU KNOW?

In 1912 Sofi Tucker began selling shea nuts at the market in Sierra Leone, West Africa. She later expanded to sell shea butter, black soap, and other homemade beauty products. Her hard work and dedication inspired the next generations of her family to create the beauty company Shea Moisture.

CELEBRATING BLACK EXCELLENCE

Houston White began selling T-shirts from his backpack when he was a kid in North Minneapolis, Minnesota. As an adult, he opened a barbershop and created a clothing line that showcases Black creativity, history, and self-expression.

White's message has inspired others to join him in creating an economic hub in the Camden neighborhood of North Minneapolis. Their goal is to support Black-owned businesses and promote cultural preservation. He also cofounded a local coffee shop, The Get Down Coffee Co., in 2021 and leads housing development efforts in his community.

REFLECT

Who are the business owners that inspire you?

SUCCESSFUL YOUNG BUSINESS OWNER

Moziah Bridges shows that age does not define the ability to be a successful business owner. He founded his own company, Mo's Bows, in 2011 when he was nine years old. In 2013 he appeared on *Shark Tank*, a TV show where business owners try to get money for their businesses. He has since worked with one of the show's judges, investor Daymond John. John mentored Bridges as he expanded his business and brand internationally.

In 2015, at the age of almost fourteen, Bridges was the fashion correspondent—someone who reports on fashion trends—for the NBA Draft. *Fortune* magazine listed him on 18 Under 18, a list of young innovators. And *Time* magazine twice named him on their 30 Most Influential Teens list. He inspires other youths to start their own businesses.

Moziah Bridges (*right*) with his *Shark Tank* mentor, Daymond John

> "I'm living proof that you can be anything you want—at any age."
>
> —MOZIAH BRIDGES, FROM HIS PERSONAL BRAND PITCH

Bridges sports a bow tie at a 2018 event.

A 1990 copy of *Black Enterprise* magazine

CHAPTER 3
MEDIA LEADERS

Black media, such as newspapers, magazines, television, and radio, provides key information about politics, business, and other issues impacting the community. Media can also highlight trends in beauty and fashion.

PAVING THE WAY

John H. Johnson and his wife, Eunice, made a pathway for Black news in mainstream media. They created *Ebony* magazine in 1945. It became a staple in the homes of Black families nationwide and at its height sold almost 2.5 million copies per issue. In 1951 the Johnsons then formed a weekly news magazine, *Jet*.

The Johnsons are widely regarded as one of the most important Black magazine publishers in US history. Eunice Johnson also built the Ebony Fashion Fair and ran it for over fifty years. The fair was the first of its kind to hire Black models and showcase high-end fashion targeting the Black community.

John H. Johnson (*left*) and Eunice W. Johnson (*second from right*) attended many events such as this gala.

A JOHNSON PUBLICATION ⊙

EBONY

THE BLACK REVOLUTION

AUGUST 1969 60c

SPECIAL ISSUE

A 1969 edition of *Ebony* magazine

PROMOTING BLACK BUSINESS

In 1970 Earl Graves Sr. launched *Black Enterprise* magazine to promote business ownership and inspire future Black business leaders. Graves recognized the importance of business in building strong communities. The magazine showcases Black-owned businesses and tools for success, encouraging and informing the next generation of Black business leaders.

Earl Graves Sr. with his book shortly before its April 1997 publication

In 1997 Graves wrote a book called *How to Succeed in Business without Being White*. It provides resources for building successful Black-owned businesses.

"My goal was to show them [other Black business owners] how to thrive professionally, economically, and as proactive, empowered citizens."

—EARL GRAVES SR. IN *HOW TO SUCCEED IN BUSINESS WITHOUT BEING WHITE*

TRAILBLAZER IN MEDIA

From childhood, Cathy Hughes wanted to be on radio, sharing stories from the Black community. With hard work, she made this dream come alive. Hughes started working in radio in 1969 in her hometown, Omaha, Nebraska. In 1971 she became a professor at Howard University. Nine years later, she bought the WOL-AM radio station and launched a talk radio show highlighting issues impacting the Black community.

Hughes made history in 1999 by becoming the first Black woman to chair a publicly traded company, Radio One. She partnered with her son, Alfred Liggins III, to expand to about sixty radio stations across the United States. She also expanded into television with the launch of the channel TV One in 2004.

Cathy Hughes speaks at a Radio One event.

REFLECT

What are some businesses that you would like to see in your community? Why are they needed?

LEGACY OF BLACK ENTERTAINMENT

Robert Johnson and his then-wife, Sheila Crump Johnson, launched Black Entertainment Television (BET) in 1980. Their goal was to reach the Black community. It began with just a few hours of programming on another network. By 1983 it became its own network. It features Black sitcoms, music videos, and other content that reaches about ninety million households. In 2001 the couple sold BET to the company Viacom for nearly $3 billion.

Singer King Combs performing at the 2022 BET Hip Hop Awards

DID YOU KNOW?

In 2013 hip-hop artist and music producer Sean "Diddy" Combs founded Revolt TV, a music and news TV network. Combs wanted to inspire, educate, and empower the next generation through music culture. Revolt hosts interviews, educational content, and more.

Sean "Diddy" Combs performing in 2022

Virginia Ali cofounded Ben's Chili Bowl.

CHAPTER 4

UNITY THROUGH FOOD

Black restaurant owners use food to celebrate the rich cultural heritage of Black Americans. Dishes such as gumbo combine West African traditions with new flavors and ingredients. The restaurants also serve as community hubs.

QUEEN OF CREOLE CUISINE

Leah Chase helped turn Dooky Chase's, a local sandwich shop, into a globally recognized Creole restaurant. Her husband's family founded the restaurant in 1941. It became a place for the community to organize for social change. The Reverend Dr. Martin Luther King Jr. and other civil rights leaders met at the restaurant throughout the mid-1900s to make plans for advancing racial equality.

Chase wanted to create a fine dining experience for the Black community while showcasing arts and culture. With Chase's

Leah Chase shares a hug with Barack Obama. Many government officials have visited Chase's restaurant.

leadership, the restaurant became the first New Orleans art gallery to showcase only Black artists. Former president Barack Obama has dined at the restaurant, along with countless other leaders and celebrities.

HOME OF THE CIVIL RIGHTS MOVEMENT

Ben and Virginia Ali founded Ben's Chili Bowl in 1958 in Washington, DC. The Ali family supported the civil rights movement of the 1950s and 1960s. They donated food to marchers during 1963's March on Washington.

The Alis also fed protesters in the Poor People's Campaign in 1967 and 1968. This movement in DC challenged politicians to take action for economic justice. The Alis made Ben's Chili Bowl a safe meeting space where organizers of this and other movements could enjoy a bowl of chili and hot dogs.

Protesters during the 1963 March on Washington

REFLECT

How can a business impact social change in a community?

COMMUNITY BAKERY AND CULTURAL GATHERING PLACE

Idris Conry opened his business, Abu's Homestyle Bakery, in 2001 to offer his community a gathering place where they can enjoy traditional navy bean pie. The pie became popular in the 1930s because of Elijah Muhammad, founder of the Nation of Islam, who urged his followers to eat navy beans. Its recipe is unique to the American Muslim community.

Conry's bakery celebrates that history. He is known in Brooklyn, New York, for serving tasty desserts from the staple bean pie to red velvet cake. His desserts have made the bakery a favorite in the local community.

Idris Conry in his business, Abu's Homestyle Bakery

MORE BLACK BUSINESS LEADERS

Black business owners impact their communities in many ways. From food to fashion, they celebrate their culture, uplift the economy, and create change.

Black business leaders such as Robert F. Smith continue to open doors for future Black business owners.

GLOSSARY

chair: to lead a meeting, group, or event

economy: the way goods and services are made, sold, and used in an area

network: a group of connected radio or television stations

net worth: how much money a person has minus debt

philanthropist: a person who donates time, money, and resources to improve the lives of others

preservation: the effort of keeping something such as culture from being lost

self-expression: showing one's beliefs or feelings through words or actions such as making art

venture capital: money invested in a business to support its growth

SOURCE NOTES

14   "Moziah Bridges," Natfluence, accessed August 2, 2022, https://natfluence.com/interview/moziah-bridges/.

19   Earl G. Graves, *How to Succeed in Business without Being White: Straight Talk on Making It in America* (New York: HarperBusiness, 1997), 16.

READ WOKE READING LIST

Ben's Chili Bowl
https://benschilibowl.com

Black Entertainment Television Facts for Kids
https://kids.kiddle.co/Black_Entertainment_Television

Bridges, Moziah. *Mo's Bows: A Young Person's Guide to Start-Up Success*. New York: Running Press Kids, 2019.

Britannica Kids: Oprah Winfrey
https://kids.britannica.com/kids/article/Oprah-Winfrey/574597

Denenberg, Dennis, and Lorraine Roscoe. *60 American Heroes Every Kid Should Meet*. Minneapolis: Millbrook Press, 2023.

Dixon, Robert P., Jr. *Gumbo Joy*. Saint Paul: Planting People Growing Justice, 2022.

Sean Combs Facts for Kids
https://kids.kiddle.co/Sean_Combs

Tyner, Dr. Artika R. *Black Achievements in Activism: Celebrating Leonidas H. Berry, Marley Dias, and More*. Minneapolis: Lerner Publications, 2024.

INDEX

PHOTO ACKNOWLEDGMENTS

Image credits: Randy Shropshire/Stringer/Getty Images, p. 4; 10'000 Hours/Getty Images, p. 5; Per-Anders Pettersson/Getty Images, p. 6; Lisa Maree Williams/Stringer/Getty Images, p. 7; Frederic J. Brown/Getty Images, pp. 8, 10; Vespasian/Alamy Stock Photo, p. 9; Johnny Nunez/Getty Images, p. 11; Bennett Raglin/Getty Images, p. 12; Leon Bennett/Getty Images, p. 14; WENN/Alamy Stock Photo, p. 15; MPI/Stringer/Getty Images, p. 16; Bettmann/Getty Images, p. 17; Retro AdArchives/Alamy Stock Photo, p. 18; AP Photo/Bebeto Matthews, p. 19; Ben Rose/Stringer/Getty Images, p. 20; Prince Williams/Getty Images, p. 21; AP Photo/Chris Pizzello, p. 22; The Washington Post/Getty Images, p. 23; Emmanuel Dunand/Getty Images, p. 24; Pictorial Press/Alamy Stock Photo, p. 25; James Leynse/Getty Images, p. 26; Pacific Press/Alamy Stock Photo, p. 27. Cicely Lewis portrait photos by Fernando Decillis.

Design elements: Anastasiia Gevko/Shutterstock.

Cover: Jerritt Clark/Stringer/Getty Images (Moziah Bridges); Jon Kopaloff/Stringer/Getty Images (Oprah Winfrey).

Lerner Publications Company
An imprint of Lerner Publishing Group, Inc.
241 First Avenue North
Minneapolis, MN 55401 USA

For reading levels and more information, look up this title at www.lernerbooks.com.

Main body text set in Aptifer Sans LT Pro.
Typeface provided by Linotype AG.

Editor: Lauren Foley **Designer:** Kim Morales **Photo Editor:** Annie Zheng

Library of Congress Cataloging-in-Publication Data

Names: Dixon, Robert P., Jr., author.
Title: Black achievements in business : celebrating Oprah Winfrey, Moziah Bridges, and
    more / Robert P. Dixon, Jr. ; Cicely Lewis, executive editor.
Description: Minneapolis : Lerner Publications, [2024] | Series: Black excellence project
    (read woke books) | Includes bibliographical references and index. | Audience: Ages
    9–14 | Audience: Grades 4–6 | Summary: "Starting a business can help meet the
    needs of a community and even preserve culture. Learn about Black businesspeople
    who have started fashion lines, restaurants, TV networks, and more"— Provided by
    publisher.
Identifiers: LCCN 2022038277 (print) | LCCN 2022038278 (ebook) | ISBN 9781728486659
    (library binding) | ISBN 9781728499970 (paperback) | ISBN 9781728496184 (ebook)
Subjects: LCSH: African American businesspeople—Juvenile literature. | Success in
    business—United States—Juvenile literature.
Classification: LCC HC102.5 .D58 2023 (print) | LCC HC102.5 (ebook) |
    DDC 650.1092/396073—dc23/eng20230119

LC record available at https://lccn.loc.gov/2022038277
LC ebook record available at https://lccn.loc.gov/2022038278

Manufactured in the United States of America
1-52596-50769-1/13/2023